4138

631.4 Heady, Eleanor B.
H
    The soil that feeds
    us

DATE			
DEC 3 '79			
MAY 20 '81			
JAN 19 '99			
SEP 27 2010			

A Stepping-Stone Book

The Soil That Feeds Us

by Eleanor B. Heady

Illustrated by Robert Frankenberg

Parents' Magazine Press • *New York*

Text Copyright© 1972 by Eleanor B. Heady
Pictures Copyright© 1972 by Robert Frankenberg
All rights reserved
Printed in the United States of America
ISBN: 0-8193-0537-5
Library of Congress Catalog Card Number: 72-171539

Contents

Chapter 1

Soil Is Important

Soil covers most of the earth. Only oceans, lakes and rivers, bare rocks, and stony mountain peaks have no soil on them.

Soil is the outer layer of the earth where forests, lawns, vegetable gardens, flowers, and wheat fields grow. Roads and houses, city streets, and sidewalks are built into and on top of the soil.

Life on earth could not go on without soil and all the things in it. The plants that grow in it feed people and other animals. Of course, fish eat plants and animals from oceans and streams, but all other life depends on soil.

Soil contains *minerals*—potash, phosphorus, and others. You can't see the tiny pieces of minerals in the soil, but they help feed plants so that the plants can grow, bloom, and make seeds. Plants store food in their leaves, stems, fruits, and seeds. Then we eat the plants—such as the leaves of spinach and lettuce, the seeds of beans and wheat, the fruits of berry bushes and apple trees. Can you think of other plant parts we eat? Perhaps you sometimes eat roots for lunch or dinner.

Cows that give us milk eat grass and hay. Hay is made from dried plants. Cows also eat grain, the seeds of some kinds of grass. The meat we eat is the flesh of animals who first ate plants to make them grow. The plants that feed animals must have soil to grow.

Roots reach down into the earth. Because they are set, or *anchored,* in the soil by their roots, plants stand up straight.

Have you ever seen a very large tree that a strong wind has blown down? Perhaps the tree was partly rotten and so fell easily. Notice how the roots spread out in all directions. Because of soil, there was a place for these roots to grow. They held the tree in place. Some trees seem to grow in solid rock. Trees may grow over rocks, but their roots always reach down into the soil.

You live in a house, perhaps an apartment
house in a city. Maybe your house is in the
suburbs, a small town, or in the country. But
wherever you live, your house sits on a
foundation on top of the soil. Perhaps it has a
basement dug into the soil.

Many animals make their homes in the soil. Larger animals tunnel and burrow through the earth. They hollow out nests and raise their children in the soil. Do you know of any animals that live underground?

The green grass in our parks and on lawns, the plants, trees, and wildflowers on our roadsides, the flowers in our home gardens, all grow in soil.

If you live in the city, you may have a
window box where you grow flowers. Perhaps
you have soil in a flower pot on your window sill
with a geranium or petunias growing in it.

The trees in our woods and forests reach tall into the sky because they get minerals from the soil. The sturdy trunks of trees are wood. We use wood in many ways. Some houses are built of wood. Even brick and stone houses have wood inside–doors, window sills, floors, and cupboards. Can you think of other things we use every day that are made of wood?

Much of our clothing is made from cotton. Machines pick the fuzzy white cotton seed *bolls,* or pods. They remove the outside coverings and the seeds, then spin the fuzz into thread. Then other machines weave it into cotton cloth.

Cotton plants grow in soil. So does *flax.* Fibers from the stems of flax are used to make linen cloth.

Perhaps you have seen sheep *grazing,* eating plants, in pastures. If there were no soil where plants could grow, there would be nothing to feed the sheep that give us wool.

Soil is truly wonderful because in it grow plants to feed and clothe the people of the world, to feed its animals, to build its houses, and to make its cities, towns, and countryside beautiful.

Some of our warm winter clothing is made from wool, which grows on sheep. Their bodies are covered with a thick, warm layer. In spring, men *shear,* or cut, the wool from the sheep, just as the barber cuts our hair. Then they wash the wool, spin it into yarn, and weave or knit it to make coats, blankets, and other warm winter things.

Chapter 2

Soil Begins

Billions of years ago the earth was solid rock. Rain and snow fell upon it. The drops slowly wore away tiny bits from the stony surfaces.

Wind blew against the rocks. Sometimes it brought with it grains of sharp sand that helped grind big rocks into smaller and smaller pieces.

Water from rain and snow seeped into cracks in the rocks. When the weather turned cold, this water froze. When water freezes it *expands,* or grows larger. This frozen water, or ice, forced the cracks apart and broke off more rock.

When the weather warmed each spring, the

snow and ice melted. Water ran from the rocks,
carrying worn and broken bits with it. Down the
hills and mountains rushed the streams, grinding
the rock pieces as they dashed against each other
and the rocks of the mountains. When the
running water reached low places, it slowed, and
the rock pieces sank to the bottom to make
sand layers.

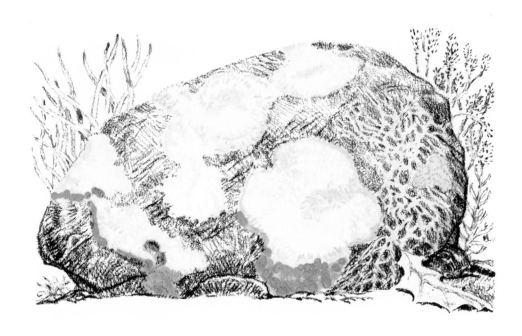

Winds blew against the rocks, bringing dust from other places. The dust caught in low spots and cracks and was moistened by rain. There tiny plants, called *lichens,* began to grow. They clung closely, almost like parts of the rocks themselves.

Lichens look like yellowish, grayish, or greenish scale, not at all like ordinary leafy green plants. Some lichens are like orange rust. Next time you are in the park or the country, look for lichens on rocks.

Lichens helped crumble the rocks into sand. As they grew, their rough scales collected more dust from the air. Lichens give off a gas called *carbon dioxide,* which joins with water to make a very weak *acid.* This acid eats into rocks, making them crumble faster.

Rain, wind, snow, lichens, freezing, and thawing continue to help turn rocks into sand. All these things together are called *weathering.*

Weathering goes on and on, grinding, breaking, and wearing rocks into smaller and smaller pieces.

Sand is the beginning of soil, but it is not yet true soil. Other things must be added to sand before plants can grow in it.

Chapter 3

Animals Help Make Soil

Weathering goes on for millions or even billions of years, turning the rocks into sand. Very gradually animals and plants come to live in the sand.

Animals dig their holes and tunnels in sand. Insects come to live in and on it. Their wastes and dead bodies rot, or *decay,* and mix with the sand. As this happens the sand becomes more like soil.

Perhaps you have seen some of the animals that help make soil. A few of them are large. Many are very, very small.

Ground squirrels, gophers, and badgers dig into the soil to make their nests. Maybe you have a dog who likes to dig holes. All digging animals stir and mix the soil.

GROUND SQUIRREL

WOODCHUCK

GOPHER

BADGER

21

Whether you live in a city or in the country, you can find some place where you can dig. Choose a damp place where the soil is loose. Dig into the earth. Do you see anything besides soil? Do you see any moving things in the soil—crawly, shiny pink things? They are probably earthworms, which spend most of their lives burrowing through the soil.

Earthworms are some of the most important soil animals. They eat parts of decaying plants that they find in the upper layers of the soil.

The worms *digest,* or use, the plant parts they eat. The wastes they leave behind help make a better place for plants to grow. Earthworms stir the soil, leaving it fine and light so that roots can push down through it. Their holes let water and air into the soil. To grow, plant roots must have water and air. When earthworms die, their bodies decay and become part of the soil.

Insects live in the soil, too. If you move a piece of rotten wood in a damp place, you may see them. They chew plants and dead wood and help turn them into soil. The top layer of soil is a network of crawling creatures. *Sowbugs* and *millipedes,* which look like worms with many legs, live and die in the upper layer of soil.

Can you think of other insects or animals that make their homes in the soil?

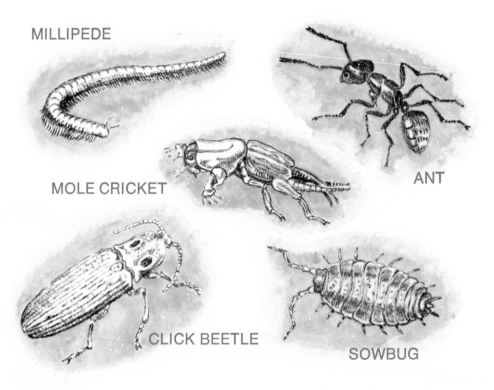

MILLIPEDE

ANT

MOLE CRICKET

CLICK BEETLE

SOWBUG

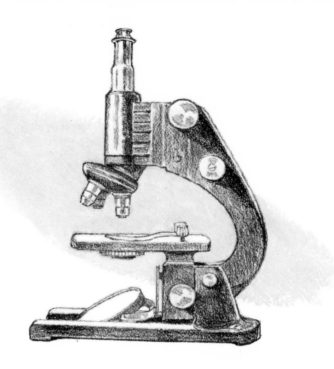

Besides all the animals and plants you can see, millions of very tiny animals and plants live in the soil. They are so small that you must look at them through a powerful microscope to see them at all. The tiny animals and plants that live in the soil are called *micro-organisms,* because they can be seen only with help from a microscope.

All the animals that live in the soil help make it a good place for plants to grow. Good soil is alive with animal life of many kinds. One small clod contains thousands of tiny micro-organisms and perhaps a few worms and insects.

Chapter 4

Plants Help Make Soil

Wind blows plant seeds onto sand. Perhaps a flying bird drops a seed or an animal drops grass seeds and burrs that have caught in his fur. When rain falls, these seeds take root and grow. Perhaps they die before they are very large, for sand is a poor place for plants.

When the plants die, their leaves, stems, and roots add to the sand, making it more like soil. Animals come to eat the plants, add their wastes, and stir the mixture.

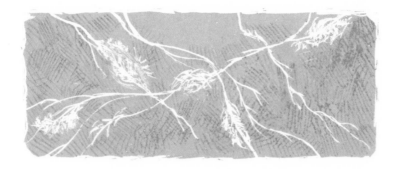

If you dig into the soil, you can see the roots of grass and trees. These are large plants. But there are tiny plants in the soil, too.

Have you seen white lines that look like hairs in dark, wet soil? These are *fungi,* close relatives of mushrooms.

Besides fungi of many kinds, soil contains millions of other tiny plants. They are not green like most plants. Some of them are much like animals. The smallest of these are called *bacteria.* You must look through a microscope to see these tiny plants in the soil. Along with the smallest animals, they are also called micro-organisms.

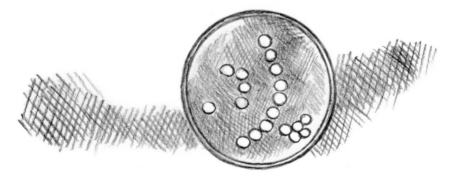

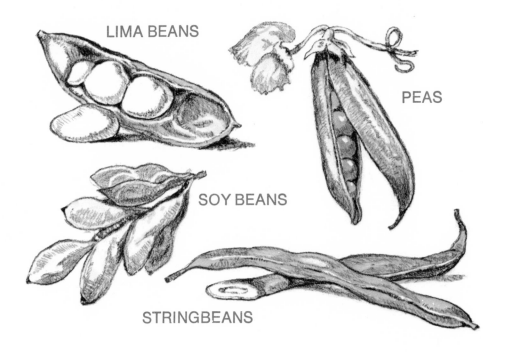

LIMA BEANS

PEAS

SOY BEANS

STRINGBEANS

Soil bacteria are very important because they help to change minerals so that soil water can dissolve them for plants to use.

One kind of bacteria takes *nitrogen,* a gas, from the air in the soil. It helps the nitrogen to join with other minerals. These bacteria, called *nitrogen fixers,* cause the nitrogen to make tiny bumps, *nodules,* on the roots of plants called *legumes.* There are many kinds of legumes. Beans and peas are some of the best known.

After the nitrogen forms into nodules, it can be dissolved by water and used by plants to help them grow strong and green.

As more and more plants grow and add their parts to the sandy soil mixture, more animals come to eat the plants. So animals depend upon plants and plants depend upon animals and all depend upon and help build the soil.

Plant and animal material in soil is called *humus*. Humus makes soil light and spongy, so it can hold the water that is necessary to dissolve the minerals to feed plants.

Soil with lots of humus in it is called *loam*.

Weathering, plants, and animals all work together to gradually build up a layer that is true soil. It may take hundreds of years to make a thin layer of soil where the climate is cold and plants and animals grow and decay slowly. In warm climates plants grow and die quickly. Animals may decay in a few days. There, the humus layer builds up in a shorter time.

Chapter 5

Soils Are Different

Perhaps you have a sandbox at home or at school. Maybe you play in sand in the park or on the beach. You know now that sand is not true soil, but only the beginning of soil.

Sand mixed with a small amount of decayed plants and animals makes sandy soil. This kind of soil is often dark on top, but light-colored just below the surface. Next time you are out in the country, look for some sandy soil. Beaches are pure sand, but back away from the strip next to the water is sandy soil.

Did you ever walk in the park or in the country just after a rain? If you slipped off the footpath, you may have stepped into mud. Perhaps it clung to your feet in great gobs, until you could hardly move. Mud that sticks like glue is mostly *clay*.

Clay soil has little humus in it. It is made of very finely ground or powdered rock or sand. When clay dries, it hardens, almost like the rocks from which it came. Wet clay is sticky. Pure clay, mixed with water, can be shaped.

Potters use clay to make bowls, flower pots, many kinds of dishes. After wet clay is shaped, potters bake it to make it very hard.

Clay must have humus added to it to make good soil for growing plants. Soil that is mostly clay is poor for farming or gardening. It is solid and without spaces for air and water. When it gets wet, it dries out very slowly.

Have you ever seen a muddy creek or river, or muddy water running in gutters at the sides of city streets? The water is muddy because there are bits of fine sand, clay, or humus floating in it.

33

Where the water runs fast, the sand and other things ride along. They hitchhike on a downhill journey. The water churns and dashes against rocks and curbings. The particles that muddy the water break into smaller and smaller bits.

When rushing streams slow down, these riders sink to the bottom or catch along the banks.

They build up a finely mixed soil layer called *silt*.
Some of the world's best farmlands are deep
layers of silt, a finely ground mixture of all the
things that make good or *fertile* soil. These soils
are found in river valleys where floods have left
their loads of silt season after season.

Try mixing some soil with water in a glass jar.
You get muddy water. But let the jar stand a
few hours or overnight. What happened? That is
the way silt sinks in streams.

Have you ever watched workmen dig a
basement to build a house? Notice that the top
layer of soil is a different color, usually blacker
than the soil below it. That black top layer,
which has humus in it, is called *topsoil*. It is in
this layer that plants grow.

Below the topsoil notice how the color changes. The soil may be sandy or full of pebbles or it may be mostly clay. The layer under the topsoil is called *subsoil*. And down under the subsoil, often very deep in the earth, is solid rock, called *bedrock*.

When soil is very wet it is quite different from when it is dry.

Sandy soil dries quickly because water runs between the sand grains. Air spaces in sandy soil are very large. Rain that falls on sandy soil drains down into the subsoil.

Clay soil dries slowly because it is made of very fine closely packed bits that hold water. There is little space for air in clay soil.

Good topsoil holds water like a sponge. Bits of humus in it soak up the rain. It also holds air, because it is light with many spaces in it. Because water helps feed plants, and the air pockets make room for their roots, the best plants grow in good topsoil or *loam.*

There are many different kinds of soil in the world. The rocks from which soils begin are made of different minerals. Soils may be formed in hot climates, on hillsides, or on flat country. All these things, and others, make soils different.

Perhaps you can collect some samples of soil. Get some sand from a sandbox, some clay, and some loam from a park or field. Put a handful of each into a separate glass jar. See how different they look.

Now add a little water to each kind of soil. Take a bit of each into your hand and squeeze it to make a ball. Feel how spongy the topsoil is. See how the sand falls apart, while the clay sticks together in a gluey ball.

Add more water to each soil sample. Then leave your jars for a few hours. Which kind of soil settles, or sinks to the bottom, first?

Chapter 6

Rich Soil and Poor Soil

A farm or garden that has rich soil can grow good plants. Of course there must always be enough water to dissolve the minerals in the soil.

Have you ever wondered why grass grows tall and green in one place and is short, thin, and yellow in another? If the water supply is the same in both places, then the soil is probably different. Soils that contain the most living things and the most decayed plant and animal material are best for most plants.

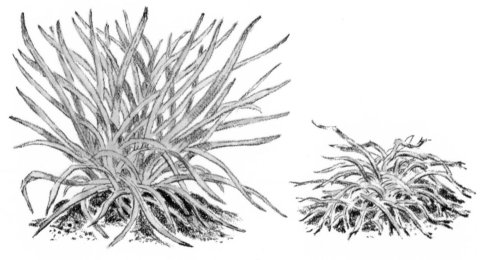

Soil that is good for growing one kind of plant may not be the best for another. Why do you suppose farmers grow corn in some places and only apples in another? Soil is part of the answer.

Sandy soil is good for growing melons or potatoes, but soil that is mostly humus is better for asparagus.

Scientists who study soils can test a sample from a field, a garden, or a window box and tell what will probably grow best there. These soil scientists help farmers plan crops so that the layer of topsoil does not disappear. In a later chapter we will find out some of the ways farmers save topsoil and make it better.

As you go to different places, collect different kinds of soil. Take some sand from the beach or a sandbox. Get another sample from a plowed field, another from a clay bank or road cut, and still another from a forest or from under a tree in the park. Cut four waxed-paper milk cartons through the middle. Wash the lower halves and dry them. Then use them for pots. Put about four inches of sand in one pot, four inches from the field in another, four inches from the clay bank in the third, and four inches from the forest in the fourth. Label each pot so you won't forget which soil is in each.

Now get some seeds. Dry beans are good

to use. Plant three seeds in each pot, about 1½ inches under the soil. Water your pots thoroughly and set them on a sunny, warm window sill. Be sure to put a saucer or lid under each pot so that water does not run through to stain the sill.

Watch for the green shoots to push their tips through the soil. The two halves of the bean will come up on a stalk. Then two tiny leaves will grow. Keep the soil damp. After a few weeks, notice which soil has grown the best bean plants. Why do you think that soil was better than your other samples?

Chapter 7

How Soil Feeds Plants

If plants are to grow strong and green, they must get a good supply of minerals from the soil.

Rain falls on the earth. It trickles into the soil. There the minerals dissolve and mix with water.

Plant roots soak up, or *absorb,* the minerals and water. This mixture moves slowly up through the plant stems to the leaves. There, with the help of *energy,* or heat and light from the sun, and carbon dioxide from the air, the green leaves make food from the soil minerals and water. This is called *photosynthesis.* The food that plants make helps them to grow larger, to bloom, and to make fruits and seeds. Plants also return *oxygen* to the air. All animals, including humans like yourself, must have oxygen to breathe.

So it is that soil, water, air, and sun work together to help plants grow. Then the plants feed people and other animals so that they can live and grow.

Perhaps you would like to see how minerals rise through plants. Try to find a white daisy. In the city, a florist might give you one. Place a little water in the bottom of a jar or glass. Color

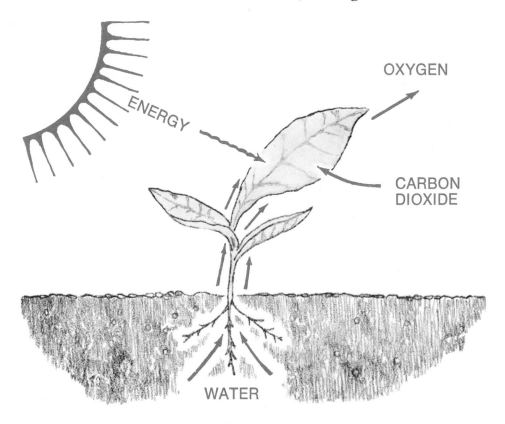

ENERGY

OXYGEN

CARBON DIOXIDE

WATER

this water with cake coloring—red, green, or blue. Be sure to use a lot of coloring.

Now take a pair of scissors and cut a tiny bit off the daisy stem. Put the daisy with the freshly cut stem-end into the colored water. Leave it in the jar for a few hours or overnight.

Now look at the daisy. It's like magic, isn't it? The flower is no longer white, but colored like the water. The daisy has lifted the colored water up into its blossom. It has absorbed the color, just as the roots of plants absorb soil minerals dissolved in water. This process is called *osmosis*. We can see the cake coloring, but we cannot see the minerals that feed plants.

Chapter 8

Soil Erosion

Soil is always changing—moving, breaking up,
blowing away.

When rain falls onto the earth it splashes tiny
bits of soil around. Clods break into smaller and
smaller pieces. Hard rain beats on the earth and
packs the soil down. Watch as rain falls on bare
soil. Notice how the drops splash when they hit
the soil—muddy splashes.

If you have a window box with soil in it,
watch through the glass the next time it rains.
If the rain falls hard enough, some of the soil
will splash up onto the sill. Then the rain will
wash the soil away into the street, where it will
be carried as muddy water down the city gutters.

During a hard rain, streams run across the land. Rushing water carries topsoil with it. It washes deep cuts, called *gulleys*. All this splashing, moving, and carrying away of soil is called *water erosion*.

Soil from window boxes, parks, and fields
moves downhill. It slowly settles in or along
streams as silt. Sometimes it is carried into big
rivers and out into the oceans, lost to the land
forever.

Soil erodes from steep hillsides very quickly.
Water runs downhill, roaring and rushing and
carrying a load of soil with it. This is one reason
why steep hillsides are so often bare and rocky.

Snow covers soil like a blanket. This cover keeps the soil from freezing hard. The snow usually melts slowly and sinks into the earth. But sometimes the weather warms suddenly, melting the snow all at once. When this happens, water runs off like heavy rain, washing topsoil with it.

When hard rain falls on the same place for a long time, the soil may become *leached*. The rain water dissolves minerals and carries them deeper and deeper into the soil. They sink so far down that plant roots cannot reach them. Leached soils are very poor for crops, because the plants cannot get the minerals they need to grow.

Have you ever been in a dust storm? Perhaps you have seen dust blow from a roadside on a windy day or seen a whirlwind carrying dust around and around.

Dust storms are caused by high winds which blow loose dry soil with them. Soil moves with the wind from one place to another. This is another kind of erosion, called *wind erosion.*

As wind moves soil, the soil breaks into smaller and smaller pieces. Sometimes wind robs one place of nearly all its topsoil, scattering it over many miles of countryside. Wind erodes soil most in flat country where there are no hills and mountains to stop the rushing gales. Dry soil

that has no plants growing on it blows very easily.

Drying cracks and loosens soil. Then wind blows this dry, light soil, carrying it high into the air and across the land in choking dust storms.

Rain, melting snow, wind, and dry weather all wear away or erode soil. When soil is badly eroded, farmers no longer have the topsoil to grow the plants and animals we all need for food.

But there are ways to save soil from erosion.

Chapter 9

Soil Is a Treasure

The science of soil saving is called *soil conservation.* Farmers, gardeners, and ranchers save and improve their soil in many ways. Farmers plow around and around hills, not up and down. This is called *contour* plowing. When rain falls on contoured fields, it catches in the *furrows,* or low places, left by the plow. If farmers plowed up and down

hills, the rain would run down the furrows and wash gulleys. These gulleys would cut deeper and deeper, carrying water and topsoil away from the fields.

Another way farmers save soil is by *strip cropping*. They plant a strip of grass, then a strip of some crop–all one kind of plant–like beans. The grass strip holds rain water in its spongy layer of leaves, roots, and stems and keeps the water from washing over the bean strip.

Some time when you go to the country, look for fields that have their crops planted in strips. These fields look as if they are striped with different shades of green.

Farmers often plant grass or vetch under orchard trees. Grass, or other close-growing plants, under trees keeps the soil from washing and blowing away. Crops planted to protect the soil from erosion are called *cover crops*, because they cover like blankets.

Grain, straw, and other leftover plant parts are often spread on fields. These protect the soil like cover crops while they are decaying. When they decay, they add to the humus in the soil.

Farmers spread manure from feeding pens and barnyards onto the fields. These animal wastes are very rich in plant foods and in humus.

Many of our soils do not have enough minerals to grow the best crops. Farmers add extra minerals to make the soil richer.

All the things that are added to soil to make it better are called *fertilizers*.

In parts of the world where dust storms often
blow the soil, a cover of grass or other plants
will help hold it in place.

Ranchers and farmers have learned to put only
a few cattle or sheep on the pastures of these
lands. The animals eat some of the grass, but
leave some to cover the soil. Careful use of
dry-country lands, called *rangelands,* keeps the
plant cover growing so that wind cannot blow
the soil away.

Road and highway builders plant the banks
and cuts on our roadsides with grass, trees, and
bushes. These plants spread their roots in the soil
and help hold it in place. They shade the soil so
it doesn't dry quickly. The plant cover helps
protect our roadsides from washing rain and
blowing wind. Growing plants also make our
roadsides beautiful.

Home and park gardeners do the same things farmers do to save and improve soil. They plant banks with plants just as road builders do.

Soil is one of the most important parts of our earth. We must protect it from erosion. We need to do everything we can to make it better. For in this precious, thin layer of topsoil grow the plants that feed the animals and feed and clothe the people of the world.

Look at some topsoil through a microscope. Amazing, isn't it? This mixture of bits of rock, decayed and living plants and animals, water, and air is the food and fiber factory for the whole world.

Index